COVER DESIGN BY A. ROMM

Publishers' Editor E. DAWSON; Technical Editor P. KASARIN;
to print April 2, 1937; Glavlit B10514. Printed by Printshop 21,
«Ivan Fedoroff», Leningrad.

Moroccan Girl, 1913.

ALEXANDER ROMM

HENRI MATISSE

TRANSLATED BY CHEN I-WAN

OGIZ — IZOGIZ
1937

For forty years, with unfailing zeal, Henri Matisse has explored the problems of plastic form and colour, tirelessly seeking new and ever more powerful means of expression. With Renoir dead, this great master of colour now stands out as the leading representative of contemporary French art.

In significance and extent of influence, he can be compared only with Picasso. Each has introduced new principles into painting; each is the recognized leader of a definite school of art.

In all countries Matisse has influenced artists without number.

The problems of colour, its dynamics and intensity, its expressive force and its relation to plastic form, have been so clearly and uncompromisingly stated in Matisse's art—and so often convincingly and originally solved—that for several decades past a study of his

5

work has been a necessary step for every prospective artist in mastering painting. Add to this, that the work of Matisse reflects with especial clarity some of the most important features of modern bourgeois art, and a review of Matisse's many years of activity acquires much more than a purely historical interest. He may be called a representative of extreme decorativism, which has arisen from the hedonistic conception of the function of art, from the soil of bourgeois aestheticism.

Matisse, as is well known, has also played a considerable role in modern art as a theoretician. He is one of those who write little, but whose comments on art exert a powerful and lasting influence. In clear and simple form he has outlined principles that completely correspond to the requirements of certain bourgeois strata in the epoch of imperialism. In his article «Notes of a Painter» (1908) Matisse, already a mature artist with ten years of independent work, enunciated the principles, that have determined all of his further creative activity. Discussing the general purpose of art, he resolutely proclaimed the principle of «art for art's sake», of the autonomy of art. He affirmed an art devoid of serious content. Probably no one has formulated the hedonistic view of art so decidedly as has Matisse: «What I dream of is an art that is equilibrated, pure and calm, free of disturbing subject matter, an art that can be for any intellectual worker, for the business man or the writer, a means of soothing the soul, something like a comfortable armchair in which one can rest from physical fatigue» [1].

---

[1] Notes d'un Peintre. Grande Revue, 1908.

This famous definition proclaims, of course, an art «without ideas». «I want my painting to give quiet and rest to the fatigued and overworked man», says Matisse [1].

What kind of painting best fulfills this purpose? Painting, obviously, that does not arouse unpleasant associations, that does not necessitate deep thought, that excites no strong emotions. From this it is a logical step not only to Matisse's rejection of all subject matter, but even to his refusal to depict the real life of the machine age. From the days of the first impressionists a considerable place in painting has been devoted to the theme of the great modern city and its industry. In Matisse's pictures one finds neither the city, its traffic, factories or machines, nor, finally, the real man of our day. Everything is invested with an air of unreality, is presented as a part of a fanciful world illumined by a bright and even light, where nothing important ever happens, where time seems to have stood still, where there are no events and no catastrophes, where there is no need of either thought or action.

Consistent in the extreme, Matisse banishes all the unpleasant or «banal» sides of life from his pictures. There is never anything remotely prosaic about his landscapes — there is not one study of a Paris street or a French village. He rejects these «boring» subjects for the sake of exotic luxury, and the more festive states of nature. When living in the North, he seldom pictures bad weather; when working in the South he

---

[1] (M. Sembat) «Henri Matisse» 1920.

does not show the sultry oppressiveness of heat. He consistently shuns anything exciting, any excesses: when in Africa, he is not interested in the vastness of the desert; when painting the sea, he shows no feeling of its vast expanses, but likens it to a piece of coloured silk.

Matisse has not only shunned «exciting» themes, he has never sought for themes in general; a theme or subject as such does not exist for him. In his own words a picture «must carry its complete significance in itself as such, and must produce an impression on the onlooker even before he elicits its meaning».

He finds motifs for his painting in his own house. He paints his studio, his family, a model, his pupils painting the same model. From year to year he paints the same simple themes, in endless repetition, but every time with new and daring plastic variations: a woman at a piano with a book; a model lying on the divan; children playing at draughts, learning songs, — all these are occasions for experimental painting. Matisse loves the four walls of his studio more than open spaces. He has few landscapes and even these are taken in their relation to a room interior. One of his favourite themes is a room with a glimpse of open country seen through its windows.

He draws from nature in order that later on as occasion demands he can desert her: «I know a study of a garden (painted in Morocco) which Matisse repainted three times, each time more closely approaching to decorativism, to quiet, and abstract beauty. When I saw it the first time, the vivid life put into the trees and grass amazed me; then the earth was covered

8

with a single tone, the grass was transformed into a uniform garland of lianas, the trees became trees of an earthly paradise. Now the picture gives us absolute repose» (M. Sembat).

The essential significance of Matisse's formula of «tranquillity» lies in this — that the picture should transport the observer out of everyday reality, out of real life, into an abstract self-sufficient world.

The observer must merely contemplate — he must think of nothing, remember nothing, he must be wafted into an abstract world of colour and form, extinguishing all senses but the visual. This principle is, in essence, an «escape from reality».

This is the «tranquility» that Matisse gives in his art. In his phantastic decorative world he calms the soul of the bourgeois, gives him forgetfullness of the social dangers of modern life, whispers to him of eternal well-being.

Matisse has held to his principles unwaveringly and tenaciously. It seems as if all the catastrophic and tragic events of the last few decades have passed him by and left him unchanged. He has remained true to his cult of tranquillity. The twenty years that have passed since his first programme declaration have been filled with wars and revolutions. — They have witnessed the birth of a new socialist world. But all this has not made him review his principles: he had developed them even further. Speaking to F. Fels in 1928 he says: «A picture must hang quietly on a wall. The onlooker should not be perturbed or confused, he should not feel the necessity of contradicting himself, of coming out of himself. A picture should give

9

deep satisfaction, relaxation and pure pleasure to the troubled consciousness».

This Matisse principle of an art without idea, without a subject, is a direct negation of the art of a preceding generation of artists. The 1880's—1890's were exactly the time, when the question of overcoming the influence of impressionism, of creating a more solid and synthetic art, was in the foreground, when the importance of significant themes in art took on new weight.

A leading feature of the new art of this period was its very clearly expressed social subject matter. This had a tradition of many years standing, inherited from the men of 1848 and 1871—Millet, Courbet, Daumier. It had roots springing from impressionism itself: elements of social satire in Degas' work—the clumsiness of the dancers and scene-shifters of the ballet amid the emphasised brilliance of the stage-settings — and was expressed in an even sharper form in the prostitutes and concert singers of Toulouse-Lautrec. While a central theme in the work of Meunier and several other sculptors, Steinlen and Van Gogh, is the life and labour of the workers and peasants, social themes expressed in his sympathy for the disinherited occupy the attention of the 20-year old Picasso.

This art represents the left wing of Modernism. No less brilliantly represented is the right wing, which inherits the experience of the impressionists, is their direct successor in form, but is reactionary in content. Here on the right we see reactionary attempts to revive religious art, and to attain a mystical communion with nature through colour and form, the symbolic mysticism of Odilon Redon and Gustave Moreau, and such Gauguin canvases as «The Last Supper» and «The Nativity».

As part of this development there appear the catholic pictures of Maurice Denis and his followers. In the person of Denis, the right wing has not only a fine decorator, but an outstanding theoretician and a keen critic. Denis attempts to guide the new art into the paths of classicism, preaches a return to the sound traditions of Poussin, without discarding the achievements of the impressionists. Finally, these two tendencies unite in an original way in the extraordinary creations of Van Gogh, which combine social subject matter—labour themes—with cosmic mysticism; misty socialistic ideas, petty-bourgeois humanitarianism and an idealisation of the medieval guilds. The development of Van Gogh's art exerted a powerful influence on a whole generation of artists, particularly in Germany. He himself becomes the hero of a myth, a prophet, an object of worship. All this is in the sphere of poetry. But there was also «prose» in the new movement — the art of those followers of impressionism who somewhat simplified its technique: exponents of an intimate art that depicts everyday bourgeois life Bonnard and Vuillard introduce an element of genre, a literary element, half ironic, half lyrical.

In the bourgeois art of this time a silent struggle was taking place between the formalists' conception of the functions of art and those who subscribed to an art of ideas. Formalist tendencies were most sharply expressed by the neo-impressionists, with whom at one time Matisse was closely related. Subject matter was far from being the essential basis of their art. Their leaders considered it quite as impossible to express their anarchistic ideals in their painting as Cézanne considered it impossible to paint his conservative and catholic principles. Matisse maintained an even more formalistic stand than this. In order to assert the formal value of his pictures he not only lessened the importance of subject matter but even weakened the element of representation — the connecting link with nature — and for the space of ten years he tended more and more away from realistic representation, toward ever greater abstraction. We can trace specifically how Matisse transforms a theme into a «purely colouristic», almost subjectless, non-representational painting. In 1907 — 1910, the years during which he experimented in decorative mural painting, he became actively interested in the idea of «Bacchanalia», a theme frequently treated during the Renaissance. In his picture, «The Joy of Life» he painted a round dance as a minor detail in the background. Later, this detail grew into an independent picture, «The Dance», and here it is already treated more abstractly; the formal elements of line and colour surfaces now predominate. Several times Matisse again returns to «The Dance», often reducing it to a detail of an interior — a corner of the studio, with the figures cut off by the picture frame, and each time the painter transposes the tone of the picture, treating it merely as part of a still-life.

In succeeding years Matisse continues to hold these formalistic principles, and strives never to go beyond the borders of that decorative, joyous garden which he once created.

Hedonism in Matisse's pictures expresses itself in a refined decorativism, in bright, fulsome and harmonious, colours in the selection of pleasant, idyllic subjects and themes, which create an impression of a happy and carefree life, of unchanging well-being and plenty.

Matisse's intimate manner is also characteristic of this hedonism. It is exemplified by that affection for homely interiors that is particularly strongly felt in the so-called «Nice Period» that begins in 1917. A striking example of this is offered by his «Storm», showing a smiling woman in a comfortable room, through the window of which is seen a stormy seascape — an obvious contrast of an intimate little personal world and the alien world outside.

Matisse loves luxury: the ordinary objects of every day use rarely figure in his nature-mortes. He prefers delicate vases, oriental rugs, bronzes and chased copper, luxurious costumes and jewelry, bright and gaudy textiles, exotic flowers. A mere list of the things he pictures makes it obvious that this is an art for the privileged few. In this respect Matisse breaks sharply with the traditions of the new art which, beginning in the 1850's takes unpretentious bits of nature, simple themes, and transforms them by the expressive power of colour harmony and form, and does not reject subject matter that would, according to the standards of academic painting, be considered vulgar. Such was the fundamentally bourgeois democratic art of Courbet, Manet, Degas, Pissaro and Van Gogh. In this respect Matisse is a throwback to the refined, festive and sumptuous romantic art of the time of Delacroix. No

13

less characteristic in this respect is the eroticism that we meet with in Matisse's pictures of the 1920's.

Despite all of these undoubtedly hedonistic tendencies, it is necessary to make certain essential reservations, both concerning the general character of Matisse's work and the social soil out of which it grows. We must note that Matisse is characterised by another tendency besides that of hedonism. In the first place the question arises — does Matisse really achieve that impression of calm which he considers to be his principal aim? It must be admitted that he attains this in only a few of his canvases; the great majority of them are instinct with impetuous movement, particularly noticeable in his more spontaneous creations, his drawings and still-lifes. As regards his decorative compositions, particularly of his latest period, it must be said that the observer experiences considerable difficulty in concentrating on them, in immediately deciphering his gleaming designs, and patterns of colour.

Such typical Matisse productions give one as little feeling of calm as the sight of ocean waves or wind-tossed clouds. As a result of this dynamism, the intelligent perception of Matisse pictures demands that the observer exert a certain amount of effort, which already precludes the possibility of complete and immediate enjoyment. Besides this, the natural forms of objects are modified and ciphered in this far from realistic style of painting.

In entering this phantastic world, the observer must, in the first place, learn how to approach and decipher these metamorphosed objects. The formalistic principles of the painter demand a certain amount of

14

erudition on the part of the observer, a certain knowledge of the laws of composition, etc. More activity has to be displayed by the observer in appreciating this art than is needed when viewing typically hedonistic art, as, for instance, the delicate and sensual images of women and children in Renoir's work. The dominant trait of many of Matisse's canvases of different periods is not conventional beauty but a certain brevity, conciseness, a merciless distortion of reality. Renoir's painted figures are the same as those that one likes outside the walls of the museum — but the same can certainly not be said of the deformed figures created by Matisse. Matisse wavers between truly hedonistic painting and what might be called «activising painting». This is particularly so in his later years, when he either approaches closer to the delicacy and lightness of Renoir and the clearness and elegance of Manet, or revelling in formalistic experiments ruthlessly breaks up his forms.

We see that in practice Matisse often contradicts his own formula. Thus his art is contradictory — reflecting the contradictions of the bourgeois world.

As Matisse has himself said, he caters to the business man and the intellectual worker. He is supported by well-known patrons of art — the Americans Stein and Barnes, the Russians Schukin and Morozov, who bought whole series of Matisse's canvases, and gave him orders for murals to adorn their palaces and villas. These men — extremely characteristic representatives of the active and progressive part of the bourgeoisie—were attracted in the first place by his daring experiments. They were not put off even by his «ex-

15

tremism», the undecipherability of a picture made it even more valuable (that is, for S. Schukin or Albert Barnes). There is, indeed, a certain special interest in deciphering these pictures just as there is in working out the blue-prints of a machine or a chess problem. Thus the intellectual element that Matisse begins by excluding from the content of his picture, reasserts itself, nevertheless, in the process of elucidating its form.

In times of social upheavals, when class contradictions are sharpened, some bourgeois circles particularly strive to get away to their own little private world — to the «home museum» in order to forget, for the time being at least, the unpleasantnesses and alarms of real life. In the final analysis the art that most closely conforms to the requirements of some influential progressive groups of the bourgeoisie is that which combines these two elements — hedonism and experimentation, or «formal» activisation. The interaction of these two elements defines the character of the art of both Matisse and Picasso: the former, fundamentally a hedonist, introduces the principle of «activisation» into his painting, the latter, fundamentally an anti-hedonist, nevertheless in his «rose period» and in his colourful decorative works of the 1920's, approaches the standpoint of hedonism.

Henri Matisse, was born in 1869, the son of a grain-merchant in Le Cateau, in the north of France. After graduating from the lycée he passed a year in the Law Faculty of the University after which he became a clerk in a lawyer's office of St. Quentin. There he attended the evening classes of the Latour Art School organised for textile workers. Later, upon the advice of the school instructors who recognised his talent, he entered the École des Beaux Arts, in 1892. Here, his first teacher was the then famous Bouguereau — sentimental and «refined».

Matisse was considered a good draughtsman. Some 20 years later, many, including his Russian critics, accused him of being totally unable to draw. Matisse undoubtedly received a fundamental academic training; this is shown by his studies of the nude made in the 1890's. They have both strength and confidence. Matisse liked to draw the figure with difficult foreshortenings, emphasising its mass. He remained with Bauguereau only a short time, then joined the studio of Gustave Moreau with whom he stayed for four years. This studio was a hothouse of new ideas in the very stronghold of reactionary academism.

Almost all the outstanding painters of the «left» came from Moreau's studio. Rouault, Marquet, Manguin, Camoin studied together with Matisse — all of them absolutely unlike their former teacher — a symbolist and mystic, the author of the allegoric and mythological compositions that now adorn the museum of his name. Moreau, distinguished by his breadth of view, did not hinder the experimental work of his students, but, on the contrary, gave them great freedom. He did not impose his own cult of archeology on them, but, for all this, one can suppose that his fundamental principle — an art for the elite, an art existing without the «deformities of modern life» [1] exerted an influence on the theoretical views of the most talented of his students.

Matisse felt the immediate influence of Moreau: for several years this daring innovator devoutly admires the old masters and attempts to master their technique. After the morning's work in Moreau's studio, Matisse used to go to the Louvre where he studied and copied the masterpieces of classical painting

---

[1] Moreau used to tell his students: «Work exclusively for the coming generations. Regard painting as a passionate silence».

as did Rouault and Derain. He was mainly interested in the realists — masters of intimate painting — Chardin and the Dutch painters. Besides these — partly to earn a living — he copied Fragonard, Caracchi, Philippe de Champaigne, Rafael. His excellently executed copies were bought by the government and 15 of them are even now exhibited in provincial French museums. Matisse's independently executed works of this period clearly show the influence of the old masters: these are mostly small canvases, still-lifes and interiors executed in grey, brown and dark «museum» tones. Both in form and colour, these sombre studies are absolutely unlike his latter orgies of colour. They have none of the typical Matisse expansiveness and generalisation, they are built up less on colour than on valeurs and chiaroscuro. They are finished as to detail and texture. Metals, faience, textiles are well represented in the academic way. But this period of cultivation of old fashioned painting was short lived. The influence of the modern school of painting soon penetrated the Moreau studio. Among the pupils there began a movement towards bright colour and more direct expressiveness. Great interest was aroused by the work of the impressionists, and also by Gauguin and Van Gogh. Matisse was particularly impressed by two Cézanne pictures bought and brought to the studio by his friend Lenaret. (Cézanne's canvases at that time were very cheap, he was still far from being a recognized master. In 1899 Matisse himself bought Cézanne's «Bathers»).

In the 1890's Matisse is still by no means a «left» painter. His evolution proceeded comparatively slowly.

While still at the Beaux Arts in 1896, he exhibited seven pictures at the more progressive Salon National; one of them, «Reader», painted in the style of the old Dutch masters, was bought by the French government. His work of this period makes an excellent impression on the leaders of the society — Cottet, Simon, Menard, all of them acknowledged masters who utilized the experience of impressionism, overcoming its shortcomings by a return to the tonal painting of the classic masters, and by emphasising subject matter, the poetic features of landscapes, and the expressiveness of the human face and figure. Matisse, on the proposal of Puvis de Chavannes, was elected an associate member of the Société Nationale des Beaux Arts. He was regarded as a rising young painter — a future classicist. But at this very moment Matisse became acutely conscious of the gulf that separates museum painting from modern reality. «It seemed to me that on entering the Louvre I lost the sensation of life which was of my time and that the pictures that I was painting under the direct influence of the old masters did not represent what I felt»[1].

At first Matisse draws closer to impressionism. A particularly strong influence is exerted on him by Manet both in drawing and colour (grey-rose harmonies) and even in his subjects (guitarists in Spanish costumes). In 1897 Matisse's Salon exhibit was «Dinner Table» — an openly «left» canvas painted in bright tones, with the drawing blurred. The heads of society lost interest in him: Matisse himself renounced

---

[1] Albert C. Barnes, «The Art of Henri Matisse», p. 366.

the path to a comparatively easy career and in 1899 his pictures are not accepted by the Société Nationale. In his foreword to the catalogue of Matisse's exhibition in 1907, the well-known critic Roger Marx characterised this crucial period in the following words: «Matisse preferred the path of trial, struggle and the bitter honour of satisfying himself, to success and easy fame».

At first Matisse had no easy time, had no regular income, and was often in want. At one time he was even forced to undertake ordinary plastering and painting. The Petit Palais in Paris still has plaster ceilings executed by Matisse and Marquet. This decade from 1895—1905 was the hardest in the life of Matisse, but at the same time, fertile for his growth. It is during these years that his artistic outlook gradually takes shape. He seeks for pure, harmonious combinations of spectral colour and decorative effects, but at first represents three-dimensional space, seeks, as before, to depict material, light and shade. His drawing becomes ever more energetic and expressive the more he frees his palette of dull tones.

This period is represented by still-lifes in harmonious rose and blue tones, by studies of models executed in a broad, generalised and already daring manner. In his compositions and treatment of objects one feels the influence of Cézanne. Matisse has not yet completely found his individual style; after a series of paintings in bright colours, he returns for a short time to his former grey tones. But later his colour chords become more and more melodious. In the 1901 Salon des Indépendants, his canvases prove to be the most

powerful and brilliant in colour of all those exhibited
and attract keen attention of the leading artists.
Matisse in these years attains great strength of brush-
work, powerful plastic form. According to Marquet
these years are also characterised by the strong influence of Van Gogh and Gauguin, and by a great
interest in Japanese prints. Matisse is attracted by the
bright colours of the South, he travels to the Medit-
teranean — where up to the present day he has generally lived and worked. He settles in Collioure, where
he joins Paul Signac, the leader of the neo-impressionist school, the irreplaceable president of the Salon des
Indépendants. Matisse paints the themes beloved of Sig-
nac-pinias on the sea shore executed in the pointillist
technique; his composition — «Luxe, Calme et Volupté»
hangs in Signac's villa. Towards 1904 he makes friends
with Cross, another outstanding neo-impressionist. Matisse however, paints his Collioure landscapes with
much larger dashes of colour than they do, his free
and daring drawing, confidently organised space
and emphasised movement are far removed from the
somewhat dry methodical manner of the neo-impressionists.

Later Matisse gave a negative criticism of this
school: «Neo-impressionism was the first attempt to put
order into the methods of impressionism, but it was
a purely physical attempt and carried out by mecha-
nical means. The disintegration of colour led to the
disintegration of form, of contour. The result was
a glittering surface. Objects differ from each other
only in regard to the intensity of light. Everything is
executed in the same way» (Cahiers d'Art. 1929, № 9).

22

During these years his interest in Eastern art grows. In 1903 Matisse goes to Munich to study a great exhibition of Mohammedan art, and in Collioure he finishes two excellent series of still-lifes with blue and red carpets, in which he again treats his colour and form in a more generalised and broader manner, already without a trace of the pointillist technique. In 1906, after his one-man show in the Druet Gallery, Matisse paintings begin to enjoy a considerable success; his pictures are acquired by the American collectors Steins, Cone and others.

Official recognition came considerably later. It was only in 1921 that the Luxembourg Museum bought one of his more realistically painted «Odalisques». «The Buffet» was bequeathed to the same museum by the author, in 1928.

In 1907 Matisse opened his school, attended by some 60—100 young artists from different countries. The school existed only until 1910, when Matisse discontinued it partly because it interfered with his own work and partly because his pupils too often painted in imitation of Matisse and did not seek out their own creative path.

The younger artists in these years (1900—1906) were filled with a spirit of unrest. They were no longer satisfied with impressionism, which was already publicly recognised and admitted to the museums of all countries. The younger generation repudiated illusionism and sought for «pure painting» governed only by its own laws; sought for freedom. Thus, on the basis of the growing revolt and individualism of the petty bourgeoisie, proletarianised through the pressure of the concentration of capital, the «second revolution» took place in French and world art.

In 1905 a separate hall of the Salon des Indépendants was hung with the paintings of Matisse, Derain, Friez, Braque, Rouault, Vlaminck, Marquet — paintings with stridently bright colours and simplified, expressive forms. For a large part of the public it was like an invasion of barbarians. The critic Leon Vauxcelles immediately nicknamed the new group «les Fauves» (the wild beasts) — thus the new tendency, like impressionism and cubism got its name from an accidental «boutade», not, it must be said, devoid of wit. The distorted forms and arbitrary proportions of these blazing canvases sharply contrasted with the pretty and homely pictures of intimate painters like Bonnard, Vuillard and Roussel, who but the day before had been considered as the vanguard of the moderns. This seemed to be a revolt against all discipline.

Maurice Denis, in a much talked of article, described the ideal of the new group as «exhausting and barren freedom».

Twenty-five years later the leaders of Fauvism thus describe the basic tendencies shown in this first appearance of the group.

Matisse: «Fauvism put an end to the disintegration of colour. It was a reaction against the diffusion of local colour in light. Light is not excluded, but is expressed in the harmony of intensely coloured surfaces. There is no need to struggle with nature in order to create light. One must seek an equivalent, by a detour. Otherwise one would have to put the sun behind one's pictures. The picture itself must be able to radiate light. The presence of such a quality is shown if the picture is placed in the shade and retains its values or if placed in the sun, withstands its brilliance» (Cahiers d'Art, 1929, № 5—6).

Friesz: «We strove to overcome impressionist trends, and, as the expression was in those days, make up for a lack of direct expressiveness by means of a new technique of painting».

Thus, in contrast to impressionism, the Fauves placed emphasis not on the study of nature, nor on the illusionary depiction of colour and light effects, but on the assertion of «free creation» not subordinated to nature as it appears to the eye. While the impressionists stressed the importance of the nature sketch and Seurat and Cézanne the finished easel picture — the Fauves at first tried to revive monumental painting and mural art.

In this sense the new school based itself primarily on Gauguin. The revolt of the Fauves was not directed against all discipline in art, as it seemed to Maurice Denis but against the discipline of naturalism and academism, against the extremes of plein-airism, against the representation of the slightest changes of morning, noon and evening light, against the disintegration of colour and form, against the merging of objects in colour, against common places that had become too obvious. The Fauves wanted huge canvases, vast surfaces animated with powerful decorative rhythms. This tendency towards monumentalism runs like a silver thread through the pictures of Derain, Friesz, Matisse, despite the sketchiness that at first characterised their pictures.

The famous formula stated by Emile Zola in the 1860's; «Nature seen through the temperament of the artist», they paraphrased to read: «Temperament that recreates nature». Thus they disregarded all attempts at illusion. This was a revolt against naturalism as merely a «list of natural effects». They took from reality only those elements that could become the basis of a new art.

It seemed that the artist, traveling the road chosen by the Fauves, attained unlimited freedom — he could break and distort his forms as he liked, and give them monumental power, the only law was his intuition which dictated the best methods of design. With a directness and intensity hitherto undreamt of he could express the most essential features of an object. But on the other hand, as the whole evolution of French art has shown — and in this quality lies its strength — rebel individualism was closely bound up with traditionalism.

Fauvism was a reaction against the formal amorphousness and accidental composition of the epigones of impressionism. The Fauves directed their attention particularly to the problems of construction of the picture surface and of clear cut form, which were of secondary interest to Claude Monet and his friends. They emphasised the object and its expressive significance in contrast to the impressionists who dissolved the object in space. The Fauves sought support and inspiration apart from the three great masters of post-impressionism, Cézanne, Van Gogh and Gauguin in the primitive sources of plastic form, in the anti-naturalistic art of the archaic Greeks, in the Egyptian painters, the Roman mosaics of the IV—V centuries and in the art of primitive peoples [1].

The interest in the primitives that began with Gauguin's flight to the green-gold «paradise» of the South Sea gained particular strength in these years. We must seek for the roots of this attraction of the «primitive» in the crisis of bourgeois culture, in the ideology of a worn-out class, for whom the cultural inheritance becomes a burden, and which strives to escape from the contradictions of capitalist reality into «the mystic days of yore» in order to regain there its lost harmony. The new school endeavored to find a firm basis for the art of the machine age in peasant handicraft art, in the anti-naturalistic art of the Negroes and Polynesians and in children's drawings. It sought the «eternal and unchangeable laws» of art in the primitives [2].

The Fauves did not succeed in overcoming the contradictions in their art or in creating a great plastic style. They did not really succeed in overcoming impressionist tendencies.

It is true that the criticism of the Fauves was directed against the very basis of impressionism — the

[1] It is sufficient to recall the traditionalism of innovators like Delacroix (Rubens) Courbet (the Dutch and Spanish masters), Cézanne (Poussin, and the Venetians), and the interesting fact that the composition of Edouard Manet's «Breakfast on the Grass», which to his contemporaries seemed daring in the extreme, was borrowed from Rafael.

[2] Vlaminck for example, in his book «Tournant dangereux» declares that he, and not Braque or Derain first «discovered» Negro sculpture and thus gave impetus to the development of cubism.

27

fixation of momentary and passing sensations, against the cult of spontaneity and first impressions» [1], but in reality the first and chief thing that happened was a repudiation of analytical methods in presenting colour. In the art of Matisse and other leading representatives of Fauvism, there was also preserved, from the fundamental tendency of impressionism, a dynamic, and at the same time unstable, perception of reality. Characteristic of this is the extreme emphasis on movement already noted in the work of Matisse, particularly noticeable in his dynamic presentations of still-life and in his predeliction for vibrating colour surfaces. In «Tangier», or in «Studio», space was perceived by Matisse in momentary fashion. In «The Road to Villacoublé» it is seen from a moving automobile. Marquet's landscapes have much in common with similar paintings of city life by Claude Monet and Pisarro, but he puts even more emphasis on movement than they

---

[1] «Movement, taken at a particular moment, has meaning only if we do not isolate it either from the preceding or following impression» (Matisse. Notes d'un Peintre). In the same article Matisse contrasts the impressionism of Rodin with the constructivism of Cézanne. «One must see the whole distinctly from the very beginning. I could name a very great sculptor who gives us marvellous fragments, but for whom composition means only a combination of fragments, as a result of which his expression is vague. On the other hand look at Cézanne; he has everything so well coordinated that at any distance and with any number of figures one can clearly define his forms and know exactly to which this or the other part belongs. If there is real clarity and order in a picture this means that initially this clarity and order existed in the artist's mind, or that the artist was conscious of the need for them».

do (representations of steam-boats, gliding through the water). Van Dongen draws the momentary poses of dancers, Friesz' pictures are more static in composition, but even his figures are usually in violent movement. Their composition, their construction of space is closely akin to the Japanese methods of the impressionists, particularly Degas, with unexpected points of view and even perspective effects (particularly in Matisse's interiors, both of his earlier and latter periods).

Often objects are cut short by the picture frame («Nasturtiums», Matisse; «Dancer», Van Dongen), a method obviously designed to give the impression of spatial depth. In «The Dance», conceived as a mural, Matisse gives a vigorous movement that could last only for a moment.

The Fauves are really not anti-impressionists. Like Cézanne and Gauguin they all went through a stage of impressionism, but it influenced them very much more deeply and their art is essentially an inverse impressionism, working with new means. They went even further than the impressionists. They introduced a new dynamic element, they emphasised movement in distorted two-dimensional planes. More synthetic as regards colour, Matisse extended the principles of impressionism in the sphere of form.

From this point of view a comparison between Matisse and Seurat, the neo-impressionist, is instructive. The latter carried the division of colour to the extreme, but attained really stable, monumental form in his «Bathing» and «Grande-Jatte». In Matisse, on the other hand, form and colour texture are more closely related than in Seurat (whose big volumes are, as it were, drenched in a shower of coloured confetti). As regards the light effects of the impressionists, although Matisse repudiated them at the outset, in the 1920's he returned to them and in colour even drew nearer to them.

The Fauves were not a closely linked group of artists. They issued no manifestoes or declarations. Fauvism could with more truth be described as a powerful art trend, which expressed very characteristic traits of the period. The strivings of separate Fauves were extremely contradictory, although there was a short period when they all painted in the same manner. The group included not only very strong and diverse personalities, but artists whose outlook on capitalist reality and the problems of art were very different.

In this one group we have Derain—attentively studying the classics and striving for harmony and quiet; Vlaminck, an anarchically inclined anti-militarist, a worshiper of originality, an opponent of the museums. The deeply tragic and grotesque prostitutes of Rouault— a poet of ugliness—and the flashy singers and dancers of Von Dongen; the monumental compositions of Matisse, Friesz, Braque, and the unpretentious landscape sketches of Marquet, Manguin and Laprade.

Though the group did not last long, this does not mean the influence of Fauvism was short-lived or transient. On the contrary, its fundamental elements are retained to this day in the work of Matisse, Braque, Dufy, Rouault, Friesz, Vlaminck and others. Such masters as Chagall and Soutine have developed from it and the elements of Fauvism are clearly defined in the work of several young artists of the Paris school, who by no means support the constructivist tendencies of

Cubism and Purism. Soon after its birth, Fauvism penetrated the art circles of most countries and became the starting point of German expressionism (particularly in the art of Pechstein, Nolde, Oscar Moll and others). Italian futurism, English vorticism and all the other isms of the time. Finally it appeared with great force in Russian pre-revolutionary painting in the «Bubnovy Valet» (Jack of Diamonds), «Oslinyi Khvost» (The Ass's Tail), the «Union of Young Painters» and other art groups.

But at the same time that Fauvism penetrated different countries and appeared under different forms corresponding to existing social conditions, we see the break-up of the group of original Fauves. New tendencies develop out of Fauvism, based on different understandings of the creative purposes of painting and in particular the Cézanne conception. Cézanne, as the most significant master of recent decades, was the starting point for the majority of modern artists, both for those who were his direct followers and imitators and for those who chose their own individual paths, and even for those who entirely repudiated his principles. Cézanne's conception of painting, based on the traditions of the masters of the Renaissance and baroque, as well as the experience of the impressionists, naturally became the basis of the art method of the generation that followed him. It was a question of reviving easel painting in all its completeness on a new basis, that by no means entailed either the formal imitation of the classic masters or their complete repudiation. By mastering the creative method of the Venetian school — the building up of volumes and space by

31

means of colour — Cézanne wished to inspire that heritage with a modern rationalistic conception of nature suited to the mentality of his epoch and his class.

Painting as we know it in the creations of the Venetians, El Greco, Rembrandt, Courbet and Delacroix, is conceived as an integral whole — that is, it synthesises all the elements of visual experience. It does not give an extract of nature, as in decorative painting or graphic art, but effectually depicts reality in order to express a definite idea, incarnated in plastic images. Thus the architectural and sculptural problems of space and volume, and the graphic problems of line and surface both find their solution in this art, as also does the problem of attaining the maximum intensity of colour, a problem that found its most complete solution in oriental decorative art. Integral painting stands at the boundaries of these two equally powerful means of representative art, on the one hand, sculptural, architectural, three-dimensional representation, and on the other, pure colour in two-dimensional decorative art. It is the centre and synthesis of all branches the plastic arts. One of the problems of the painter is to determine the spatial relations between objects, ascertain the contrasts of their forms, mass and proportions, the interplay of their lines. But the specific problem of the painter consists in translating these conceptions of volumes in space into conceptions of flat, colour surfaces[1]. The ordinary contrast of near and

---

[1] Matisse himself has stated that «the aesthetic emotion with which an object inspires him is never fully expressed until the object has been completely reconceived in terms of colour» (A. Barnes, o.c.p. 100).

Family Portrait, 1908.

far objects (their relation in space) must be transfromed in his mind into conceptions of objects as colour surfaces with the basic qualities of colour in definite combinations. But a higher and more complex problem is the synthesis of both these elements: the deepening and differentiation of colour, the finding of the final and necessary positions of the colour units, in order to complete that recreation of form that adequately reflects reality.

It is well known that this problem posed in a completely new and unconventional way was rather beyond the powers of Cézanne, that he was always dissatisfied with the results he obtained. Often he stopped work half way through his pictures or destroyed them, and during many years he returned again and again to the same problems which remained unsolved up to the very end.

The tragedy of Cézanne, however, does not rest in his qualities as a painter but rather in the specific problem that he set himself and the objective conditions of his time. He repudiated the formal and sham imitation of the classics bound up with the illusionism so widespread in the XIX century, and also the pseudo classicism of stylists like Puvis de Chavannes. He strove to master completely the creative methods of the XVI and XVII century masters, utilise at the same time the colour attainments of impressionism, while looking at the world in a modern way («recreate Poussin on the basis of nature») for Cézanne's perception of colour was more variegated and intense, and his perception of form more simple and dynamic, than that of the old masters.

Thus, Cézanne wanted to recreate an integral organic art on the basis of the contemporary ideology of his class, torn by the contradictions of the epoch of the decline of capitalism—that is, he attacked the problem of «Grand Art» which for modern bourgeois art is utterly insoluble.

The artists of the following generation, realising the insolubility of this problem, advanced in opposition to this too complex conception, the principle of self-limitation which played so great a role in the art both of Matisse and Picasso. Both of these repudiated the complete realisation of an art idea in the Cézanne sense. Their self-limitation essentially admits their lack of confidence in their powers and is extremely significant for modern bourgeois art.

The inheritance of Cézanne is as it were divided into two—Picasso, Braque, Derain take and develop his analysis of form, which implies distortion and reconstruction of masses in space; Matisse, Dufy and others take as the basis of their art the dominance of colour over form and the decorative elements of Cézanne. We must note, however, that these are not two completely inimical camps. As a result of further development, there appears colourful decorative cubism in two-dimensional planes; on the other hand, Matisse often utilises cubist methods.

Both tendencies are equally anti-naturalist, they strive to «overcome the natural object», that is, so to transform it on the canvas as to arrive at something completely new, perceived as pure painting, having as few points of contact with reality as possible.

This problem runs through all «left» art, but in the 1900's it was particularly strongly defined. «In a picture»—Matisse writes—«there must be nothing that can be described in words or that already exists in our memory... A picture is a real organism or it is nothing... When I see a picture I forget what it represents, all that is important is line, form and colours...» The two tendencies used different methods while striving for the same thing that is, «pure painting»[1].

While the decorativists, despite their distorted form, retain the external likeness of objects, the cubists disintegrate and reconstruct it. At a first glance this would seem to be a more radical step towards abstract painting, but in reality cubism only superficially overcomes the element of representation. The cubists overthrew the old order and set up a new one, adopted a new set of pictorial forms, supposedly abstract (but in reality met with in nature, in crystals, etc.).

The object in «pure» cubism is conceived in a very real, material way—its mass, weight, content and surface is emphasised to such an extent that abstract geometric masses attain an effect of ponderousness that literally weighs down on the observer as in Picasso's latest work.

It is obvious that we are dealing with a superficial surmounting of the object concept, a mere extension of the number of forms treated in painting. The cubists,

---

[1] Matisse never negated the value of cubism, he even considered it a «step in the direction of pure painting». The adherents of cubism regarded his painting with considerable less patience (see the views of André Salmon and other critics of the cubist camp).

when they remained true to their original ideas, limited themselves to the first stage of perception in painting as described above. In the pictures of Léger, Gleizes and Picasso of that time, architectural, graphic and sculptural elements, therefore, predominate.

Meanwhile the school of decorative painters endeavored to «surmount the object» by means of painting itself, that is, by transforming the objects into flat colour areas — a method that is obviously more organic and pictorial. This tendency does not give a synthesis, does not adequately reflect reality, but, nevertheless, it operates predominantly with the specific means of painting and can thus more naturally be a starting point for the creation of a real style of integral easel painting.

We must note that Matisse is much nearer to «objectlessness» in painting than the cubists, who essentially strove to be «more real than nature», which latter tendency finds its most extreme expression in the surrealists and in Picasso's last work. Matisse did not make a cult of the object and was even negative in his relation to it. And in fact, in creating his artificial world, his «decorative paradise», Matisse in the 1910's throws out the most essential elements of an object — its very bodiness, its density, its mass, its surface quality, the specific quality of its texture. His method means the dematerialisation of objects, but he does not arrive at this immediately. In 1907— 1908 he draws several pictures («Model» in the museum of Modern Western Art and others) where the chief problem is to show relations of masses. In these pictures he rejects bright colours, draws in black and white with reserved yellow tones, and is very close to the initial stages of cubism; but they remained isolated experiments in his creative life.

After this episode, Matisse, during the whole of his Fauve period (1908—1910), consistently follows out his hedonistic and decorative conception of art and discards those elements of painting that enable one to construct three-dimensional space. This process proceeds side by side with a search for pure intensity of colour and the simplification of the colour composition of his pictures: to begin with he discards tonality and light and shade. Matisse renounces conventional harmony in his pictures, general tonality, and in 1906, like the other Fauves, transfers his interest to local colour. Then he substantially discards the traditional laws of perspective, takes to a stylised organisation of space, discards the representation of three-dimensional volume, and correct drawing — that is anatomical verisimilitude in the drawn figure, and finally abandons the representation of different textures. Matisse at last arrives at complete dematerialisation of the objective world in his pictures of 1912, painted in Morocco. Thus he discards extremely valuable elements of painting, part of an inheritance that had been slowly developed in

European painting during hundreds of years and that had recently been reaffirmed with particular power by Cézanne. Having thus shaken off the traditions of Western colourists, Matisse firmly associates himself with oriental traditions. Oriental art, as represented both by Japanese coloured prints and the art of the Mohammedan Orient [1] is, in its fundamental aspect one of the component elements of the decorative art of Matisse.

In this art, colour harmony is not attained by toning down local colours, or by a comparative unity of colours, but by utilising a multitude of contrasting colour units, by a strident struggle of bright colours and the contrasting of ornamental surfaces. The dominance of colour over form, ornamentation and gay variety, the simplification and stylisation of objects, their reduction to flat decorative colour surfaces — all these characteristic traits of Oriental frescoes, miniatures, faiences, textiles and rugs, are present in the pictures of Matisse. But we must note that Matisse is not a direct imitator of oriental art; he is rather a follower of that art. He adopts the oriental principles of decoration, but does not for instance, stylise his figures in imitation of Persian miniatures,

---

[1] The most characteristic trait of this latter art — its abstractness, developing in the XII century into abstract ornamentation, was the result of a religious taboo (arising out of the «Hadiths» a collection of the sayings of Mohammet) that forbade the representation of living forms. Mohammedan artists either modified their figures of animals and plants so that Allah would not recognise their creations at the last judgment, or reduced them to ornamental symbols.

and he combines this oriental decorativeness with a purely Western feeling for movement.

Matisse's sojourn in the East had a tremendous significance for the further development of his art. He spent the winters of 1911, 1912 and 1913, in Morocco.

If in Collioure Matisse painted oriental rugs, after his stay in Africa, he sought to make his pictures themselves look like rugs. It is characteristic of him that while in the East he was interested not so much in the nature of the country, the landscape and the people, but in the decorative applied arts that play so large a part in the life of the East.

Orientalism is no new phenomenon. We find a deep interest in the East in the work of Carpaccio and Rembrandt (who even copied Persian miniatures). We must, however, differentiate between two ways of approaching the East — on the one hand, an interest in colonial exoticism, and on the other — a subordination of oneself to the oriental outlook on life. In the epoch of early imperialist expansion the ruling classes of the metropolis are convinced of the superiority of European culture over that of the inferior black, yellow and brown races. Then there comes the acceptance of Eastern philosophy as a powerful apology for the existing social system, and by the XIX century we have such significant phenomena as the metaphysical systems of Schopenhauer and Hartmann or the «Tristan» of Wagner. In the period of the decline of capitalism, after the wreck of all former ideological systems, we have a «crisis of thought». There begins a search for a more suitable and powerfully hypnotic ideology:

bourgeois intellectuals, who were formerly decidedly anti-religious, are now attracted by the most reactionary theories of oriental mysticism. They begin to regard the East as a source of wisdom, assume that the East has secrets and forces that are not accessible to the rationalistic European. They try to learn from it, and in this way many mystical schools and sects arise. Analogous to this is the striving of many artists to become followers of oriental art.

In the XIX century the East attracts the attention of Delacroix, Decamps, Fromentin and many others. But they approach the East with European methods of painting. They utilise it as material that can be worked up according to one or the other Western formula.

The impressionists first began to attune their Western formula to Eastern (Japanese) harmony. But the few adaptations of Japanese methods, made by the impressionists in the sphere of composition, and by Van Gogh in drawing cannot be compared to Matisse's predilection for Oriental patterns and colours for the daring, decorative arabesque.

Matisse went much further than the impressionists. He not only utilised the methods of the Oriental decorators and filled many of his canvases with Persian and Arabian patterns, but even tried to look on the world through the eyes of the ancient feudal East. See how close is his basic principle, his striving for harmony, calm and abstract beauty, free of subject matter — to the Eastern conception of an art serene, and far removed from everyday life, to the concept of quiescence and mystic contemplation, the striving either to gild reality or flee away from it, that is so characteristic of the painting and poetry of the ancient East. In such pieces as «The Arab Café» where the Arabs recline in attitudes of complete lassitude, are as it were dissolved in space, transformed into schematic ornaments of colour, this close relation is particularly keenly felt [1].

After his stay in Morocco, Matisse's compositions become even more abstract, his objects even more illusive in substance.

But Matisse also tries to depict the real East and here it must be admitted that his approach is not distinguished by originality. This is the East superficially perceived and understood, an all too usual exoticism, seen through the window of a hotel. It is of course true that the artist did not intend at all to depict the real everyday life of an Eastern city, the closeness of its streets, the bustle of its bazaars, its dust and noise, its gaudy crowds, its sharp contrasts of light and shade, rich clothes and rags, its

[1] An apt characterisation of this aspect of Matisse's compositions is given by J. A. Tugendhold: «His composition is unconfined — it can be continued both in breath and height. The many coloured patterns of his table cloths run over the canvas in a rhythmic pattern, but this pattern can be continued into space beyond the frame of the canvas. There is in his pictures a sort of freely flowing life that bursts out of them as if to spread over the wall; they seem like fragments of some unrealised frieze. Of a like character is the composition in Persian and Arabian tiles, rugs and textiles — an ornamental pattern not confined to any one place, instinct with a striving for the infinite, for the absolute. It is in this oriental thirst for the absolute, in this dissolution in contemplation that Matisse finds happiness «free of all disturbing subject matter» (The First Museum of Modern Western Art, Moscow, 1923, p. 72).

characteristic figures of beggars and coolies, bent under the weight of heavy burdens. All these are «disturbing subjects». In contrast to these expressive themes Matisse preferred a decorative and aesthetically perceived East [1].

Did Matisse compensate for the elements of Western painting that he discards? We must admit that he enriched painting with new and powerful pictorial means. After studying the laws of colour for many years and mastering to perfection the art of colour combinations, he developed a powerful new pictorial element, the fulcrum of his art. This new element is the dynamic force of colour surfaces and an extreme intensity of colour, such as had not been seen in Europe since the time of the Gothic stained glass windows. The colour reaction from Matisse pictures is very strong: this reaction is sometimes, perhaps of a negative nature, but it is always very intense. His pictures are rich and brilliant fanfares of colour that are sometimes almost deafening. They do not dispose one to calm and pleasurable admiration, they are visual

---

[1] It is interesting to compare the orientalist Matisse with two Russian artists who are to a great extent his followers and at the same time owe much to Orientalist decorative art. Saryan has given us in his pictures of the Caucasus, Persia and Egypt, an East that is bright and colourful, but more real than that of the French master. He paints the sultry sunburnt Eastern landscape, the struggle between light and shade («Street in Constantinople») depicts everyday life, not limiting himself merely to «pleasant impressions» like Matisse. In his early pictures of the Kirghiz steppes, Pavel Kuznetsov's attitude is one of idyllic contemplation that is also characteristic of Matisse's outlook on the East.

paroxysms. This is not a «feast for the eye» but a veritable orgy [1].

How does Matisse attain such strong colour effects? In the first place by sharply emphasising colour contrasts. We had best cite the words of the artist himself. «In my picture «Music» the sky is painted a beautiful blue colour, the bluest of blues, the surface is so permeated with colour that the blue is completely perceived, the idea of absolute blue; for the trees I take a pure green, for the bodies a sonorous vermilion. A particular point: form changes as a result of the reactions of neighbouring colour surfaces; for expression depends on the colour surface that is perceived by the onlooker as a whole» (Cahiers d'Art, 1929, № 9) [2].

In 1908—1912, Matisse, using almost exclusively pure colour (in rare cases he uses mixed half tones)

---

[1] Here are a few descriptions of the effect of Matisse's colouring: Paul Rivière: «Matisse's colour is static. It is as immovable as thought, a glittering, scintillating extract». Guillaume Apollinaire: «If Matisse's art needed a comparison, we should have to take an orange. Matisse's art — is a fruit of dazzling colour». In the opinion of Valdemar Georges «Matisse in his colouring is the true descendant of Delacroix». And here are examples of a negative reaction; K. Schaeffler («History of European painting»): «Colour becomes brilliant but takes on something of the nature of aniline dyes». O. Mandelstamm («A Journey to Armenia»): «On the other hand I did not like Matisse, the artist of the rich. The red colour of his canvases burns like soda. He had never known the joy of ripening fruit. His powerful brush does not enchant the eye but over-exerts it so that it is filled with blood».

[2] In one of Van Gogh's letters there is a paragraph which superficialy resembles the above description, but which clearly

44

builds up his pictures in three fundamental tones. «Satyr and Nymph» is a harmony of green, rose and blue. «Dance» is in blue, green and red; his still-lifes are built upon harmonies of lilac, yellow and red or blue, violet and rose. Later, in 1912, he changes to a four-colour harmony, in which one of the four tones in the picture is given but little space: «Tangier» — blue, orange, pink and red. «On the Terrace» is in lilac, green, rose and blue. «Gateway of the Kazbah» is in raspberry red, sky blue, green and pale rose. In later years Matisse makes use of more complex combinations and considerably enriches his palette, introducing a greater variety of tones.

Matisse justifies his method of simplifying his palette, by the well known fact that the colours at the disposal of the painter cannot compete in strength with the effects of colour and light met with in nature; therefore it is necessary to take the strongest contrasts and avoid half-tones. «In so far as I am concerned with local form, for example a leg, I must logically use a real body colour. However, I have to use vermilion: my combination of blue, red and green is sufficient to make an equivalent of the spectrum. Besides this, these three notes react on each other and give rise to shades that are not found in pure colour.

shows the fundamental difference between the symbolic standpoint of the founder of expressionism, and the formalist approach of Matisse: «I want to paint the portrait of my friend and express in it all the love I hold for him... As a background, in place of the banal walls, I will paint infinity — the most intense blue that my palette bears. Thanks to this juxtaposition, the golden head on the blue background will seem like a star in the deep blue of the sky».

45

These tones must be sufficiently vigorous in their interplay to replace the colours that are absent from the palette» (Cahiers d'Art, 1929, № 9).

Here it is important to decipher the meaning of Matisse's remarks on the mutual interraction of pure tones. Speaking of shades of colour, Matisse evidently does not have in mind the gradations of full tones — the gradual dimunition in intensity that can also be obtained by the use of pure colours (as in the Italian and Russian primitives), obviously also he does not mean the accidental shades that can be perceived by the observer as a result of the conflict of strong colour surfaces, a sort of echo of the neo-impressionist theory of the optical mixture of colours. These vibrations are too infinitesimal, and the impression of these intermediate shades is too temporary. Here he evidently speaks of the necessity of introducing transitional tones, which he actually did in practice later on.

Working as he was with pure colours, Matisse, like every other artist wants to avoid monotony — the antithesis of painting — but he is not always successful and a few of his pictures are rather monotonous (e. g. «Music»). On the other hand in the 1910's he wants at all costs to retain the purity of his colour. Avoiding the mixing of colours, he has recourse to a method that is analogous to the «glazes» of the old masters — the imposition of a light colour on a darker one, for instance, white on rose, or lilac on blue, etc. Then in order to make his colours vibrate he energetically plasters them into the canvas; instead of using white paints, he compels the canvas to shine through the layers of colour, or leaves spots of bare canvas.

Sometimes he uses layers of paint of different strength (for example in «Girl with Tulips») stressing one colour at the expense of another. Several paintings of 1912 are executed with smooth, even surfaces. If the surfaces of some of Matisse's pictures seem dry and monotonous, this by no means tokens a negligent attitude to the painter's medium, unthinkable in a great medium, but is a sign of his fear of overworking that material. For Matisse, as a decorator, the unity of the picture with its base — the canvas — is particularly important. The whiteness and structure of the latter is given as much consideration by him as a monumental painter gives to his wall. But while remembering the base of his picture, Matisse sometimes forgets about the pigments themselves, about the specific peculiarities and possibilities of oil painting.

Particularly significant is Matisse's manner of leaving his details unfinished. This is well exemplified in his «Moroccan Girl», in «Ball Game» and other canvases, where instead of making the colours duller in those places that he wants to tone down, he leaves spots of canvas bare (as he does also sometimes when he wants to show light), or leaves the details incomplete (generally the hands, legs, etc.).

In his Fauve period Matisse consciously limits himself to lustreless, liquid painting and does not pay particular attention to questions of surface quality. This is undoubtedly a shortcoming in his early pictures, particularly if we consider his many years of conscientious work with colour contrasts, and his tireless experimental work in studying psycho-physical reactions to different colour contrasts. Matisse is not

47

satisified with the system of complementary colours, discovered by Delacroix, and developed into a system by the impressionists. He seeks for dissonance, for sharp and strident colour chords — here his art can be paralleled by the modern music of Stravinsky, Strauss, and others. In him, as in these composers, we sense the alarmed and psychologically unstable, overwrought consciousness of the modern bourgeoisie. Though of late we see in Matisse an evident striving for more tender harmonies, for a deeper development of colour and greater unity.

Matisse attains unity and at the same time colouristic variety, firstly, by realising a truly organic union between colour and plastic form. Colour so dominates over form in his art, that it can be considered the real content of his pictures, and all the rest merely functions of his powerful and dazzling colour. Drawing, as such, has always for Matisse played a subsidiary role to colour; linear development has always gone parallel to the development of the colour qualities of his painting.

During the period of his first experiments, Matisse's drawing was somewhat vague and approximate («Dinner Table»), but gradually it became ever more exact and expressive. Matisse draws much and tirelessly from nature, his drawings run into the hundreds and as a draughtsman he is a real master. His extraordinary craftsmanship is evidenced by any one of his vivid, impulsive sketches from the model. Remarkable exactness is displayed in the way he places his figures on the paper. He unerringly finds the correct proportions between his forms and the flat surface of the sheet

Gold Fish, 1911.

of paper. Even his slightest sketches are conceived as compositions. They are generally executed in an expressive arabesque that cuts the paper surface diagonally. The keen vision of the painter immediately transforms a glimpse of nature into the interplay of decorative lines and surfaces without ever losing its vitality, rather, on the contrary, sharply emphasising it. Without worrying over details Matisse seizes the very essence of a movement, artfully generalises the curves of the body, gives unity and proper construction to the form.

Matisse drawings are so daring, dynamic, simple and succinct, their plastic quality is so original, that it is impossible to mistake them for the work of any other of the famous draughtsmen of his day [1].

In vitality and directness they are equal to the Japanese, in decorativeness—to the Persian miniatures, in expressiveness of line to the drawings of Delacroix.

At the same time they are by no means based on mere technical «agility», or a predilection for effective flourishes — they are constructive in the real meaning of the word, for their depiction of plastic form is completely convincing.

His unending study of drawing has made Matisse a master of the brush. The contours of his pictures are confidently traced out with one stroke of his brush.,

---

[1] We should perhaps note a certain influence of Rodin, in these drawings as in his early sculptures, but we must add that the great sculptor could hardly have found a more gifted and independant follower.

His pictures, particularly in reproduction, are often like brush drawings. Their effect is often sustained by his masterly, daring line.

The technique of his drawings is varied and he controls all his mediums to perfection. With a few lines, in his pen drawings (his favourite technique) and engravings, he models out the figure, or with a confident, delicate, nervous but at the same time

flowing and continuous line, he marks off the contours. In his lithographs, pencil drawings and dry brush work, he sometimes gives the intermediate tones with a light and transparent wash or shading, finely working out his plastic forms.

These drawings are distinguished by their fuller treatment from his pen drawings and etchings which have more the character of improvisations, at the basis of which, however, lie exceedingly nice judgment and a tremendous amount of preparatory work.

«I made some of my etchings, after hundreds of drawings, and experiments, experiments to define form.

Then I executed them with closed eyes» (F. Fels. Page 50).

But no matter how finely executed these Matisse drawings with all their excellent qualities are they do not make us forget that these are the drawings of a painter, mainly preparatory sketches, material for painting.

Often a drawing takes the place of a study on the canvas, and the same forms are painted directly into a finished picture. His drawings are always instinct with colour. The monochromy is made up for by the interplay of deepened black dashes, contrasts of fine, hardly noticeable lines with thick ones, and of late, with grey-black half tones.

One cannot forget that his drawings are not realistic, that he more closely depicts nature in his «rough» drawings and that in his more «showy» line drawings and vivid book illustrations and decorations, he uses distortion. Distortion is one of the most characteristic of Matisse's traits. He needs it primarily in order to «get away from reality», in order to create a phantastic world in which one is led away from real life.

As is well known, Cézanne in his last period, when working for a long time at a picture, constantly deepening its colour relations, often changed his drawings of the figure. In the big composition «Bathers» he changed his proportions several times. Cézanne's method of generalization and deformation was extended by Matisse into a system in 1905—1908. In 1908 the painter Devallière thus explains the idea that inspires Matisse's method: «Like our ancestors, the Romanesque sculptors who deformed their figures out of the necessity of combining them with architecture, Matisse when drawing, takes into consideration the right-angled form of the paper. If the drawing of the model is not correct — that is, does not correspond to the usual conception of the female figure in the given pose, the form for all that does not become less truthful for the size of the head corresponds to the volume of the foot and torso. These separate parts of the body are presented by the artist so that the white spaces between the edge of the paper and the black lines of the figure form an expressive ornament» (Grande Revue 1908, XII).

Matisse's distortions in these years are rather extreme, he cuts off details of anatomic forms or excessively enlarges separate parts of the body (for example, the head). Examples of this are seen in «Dance» and «Music» — that is, more finished compositions.

If we compare the early sketches of the pictures we become convinced that, as with Cézanne, his deformations develop in the process of work. Thus, it is impossible to explain them as does Devallière, exclusively as a result of consideration for lineal and surface composition. They are bound up with a specific element of painting — the dynamic quality of colour, the attempts to give vividness to a dissonance of three colour chords, to force the colour surfaces into close contact, to give the picture unity. These «désaxations» and changes that are carried to the point of absolute distortion are induced by the demands of colour composition inasmuch as Matisse primarily builds up his pictures on this latter principle.

In his drawings Matisse works with contrasts no less than in his paintings. If he uses pure colours, so he uses «pure» lines — contrasting straight, broken' angular ones with circular and elliptic, all in relation to linear-surface deformation. In his earlier works of 1905—1908 (for example in «Model»), there is a predominance of angularity, but in later years Matisse tends more and more to «Rondism» — to stylisation in circular, curved and elliptic lines. The play of contrasted lines, the balance of straight and crooked lines is clearly evident in «The Dance». The powerful curved line, running from the turned head of the first figure on the left through the preturberant hip down to the extended foot, serves as the dominant note of the picture. It gives the impression of vigorous im pulse and powerful energy. «Spanish Girl with a Tambourine» is a no less pointed example of this method, for in this composition the angular lines are concentrated on the left side of the figure and on the right as an offset to this — are elliptical lines.

Contour plays a big role in Matisse's painting. He uses it to accentuate not only form but colour, in a manner similar to Van Gogh's. For example, in «Lady on a Terrace» he surrounds the orange dress with a green contour and the yellowish green hills on the horizon with a thick red contour. In some pieces he uses a black contour only as an ornamental emphasis for form, but in others (for example «Ball Game») he uses his black as a colour, setting it off with bright spectral colours. In later pictures he willingly uses black of different shades. Sometimes, however, Matisse weakens his contours — as, for instance, in «Moroccan» where form dissolves in colour and assumes a hazy character.

This haziness or indistinctiveness is particularly evident in his many still-lifes with flowers whose colours are repeated in the patterned backgrounds.

In some pictures of 1911—1914 this extreme ornamentation based on the rhythm of patterned colour areas evolves into its opposite — into amorphousness. His pictures become as monotonous as the pictures of the neo-impressionists that he criticizes, with the only difference that dots and lines are replaced by larger patterned dashes of colour. The image itself disappears, drowned in decorative colour. By continuing this tendency Matisse is on the threshold of his secret desire, which he has so often approached, but has never decided to follow up to the end — to «pure» abstract painting, to the complete removal of concrete objectivity — that is to say, the complete negation of the representative side of painting.

Matisse was very close to this when he took his objects in a very schematised, conventional way or made them into almost abstract patterns. But the logical conclusion of his principle «that the significance of a picture must be in itself» was not drawn by him, but by Kandinsky, Malevicz and other «abstractionists».

Kandinsky, gifted with a fine feeling for colour and rhythm, striving to create absolute painting, likening it to music, gives in his canvases a combination of rather vaguely shaped colour surfaces, juxtaposed with daring lines. His painting nevertheless cannot be called «abstract» in the full meaning of the word, because he uses organic forms, like leaves and stalks, the wings of butterflies, the curves of shells, etc. In contrast to the emotional and lyrical Kandinsky, the rationalist Malevicz constructs dry compositions out of the simplest geometric forms — black squares, red circles and quadrilaterals, etc. In their creations, decorative abstract painting fell into a cul de sac, and despite the colouristic talent of Kandinsky, and Malevicz's constructivism, they did not enrich the means of painting but exhausted them. The logical result of «pure» painting is either a chaotic kaleidoscope as in Kandinsky or the Simultanists (Delauney) or extreme poverty of form, dryness and desolate schematism as in Malevich.

This pure painting finds a wider application only when it ceases to be «pure» and enters the sphere of the «applied arts» (suprematist and simultanist ornament in pottery, textile, books, posters, clothes, automobiles, etc.). Thus the circle is completed: the «pure painting» that was evolved by Matisse under the influence of the Oriental decorative arts, returns to the applied arts in a new guise. In place of the «Grand style» that was dreamed of by the abstractionists, «pure painting» is turned to the task of decorating everyday things.

We already know the ideological standpoint of Matisse so we should not be surprised to see that he reached the culminating point of abstraction during the years of the great war. At a time when some artists joined the camp of the chauvinists, and others actively protested against the war (as shown in Vlaminck's autobiographical and anti-militarist book «The Dangerous Turning»), still others preferred to retire into themselves, and get as far away as possible from the hard facts of reality. We are inclined to believe that Matisse belongs to this latter group. It is in these years of 1916—1918 that he paints several paintings, schematic in the extreme, where he uses methods that are either purely cubist or akin to suprematism.

But at the same time these years were for Matisse years of new and varied investigations. At any rate, the tragic events of the war must have exerted a certain influence on him. It was during these years that there awoke in Matisse an interest in psychology — evidenced in the expressive and tragically conceived «Female Head» (1916). Although this trend soon weakened, and appeared later in only a few canvases such as «Woman with an Aquarium», nevertheless the strivings of that period served as the point of departure for a new development.

In a preceding period Matisse really did not paint live people — the human figure like any other object was merely an accessory for the effects of painting. Besides this, in his bigger and more finished compositions, the human figure is never dominant, but on the contrary, still-life — carpets, draperies and furniture — is painted with greater strength than the human figure as in «Red Room», «The Family Portrait» or «Portrait of Madame Matisse» (1912) where the face is a dead mask, completely schematised, while the dress and the chair are accentuated.

These creations of the 1910's can be called portraits only in the most conventional sense. The lines of the face are extremely generalized, they do not convey the individual character of the model, but rather too much of the subjective state of the artist. The seemingly vital treatment of these faces and figures should not mislead one — Matisse gives his still-lifes even greater vitality. All his portraits are characterised by the same sharp, distinct, big features, treated decoratively, with one and the same intense expression. They are free of all psychologism, they tell nothing of the inner life of the model.

Between these «portraits» of Matisse and the deeply psychological portraits of Van Gogh and the young Picasso there is a great gulf. Here Matisse is deliberately superficial — he subordinates the structure of the human face to decorative rhythm.

The heroes of his pictures are average non-intellectual people. He does not try to present characteristic, interesting faces, much less does he try to show the social character of the model, which is so vividly seen in the pictures of Degas, in Van Gogh's portraits or in Cézanne's pictures of peasants. He has to fill his decorative heaven with abstract people who do not call up social and psychological associations, and so he is satisfied with a ready-made scheme that he employs unchangingly. He seems to think that by ridding the model of his individuality, he thus transfers him to a higher plane, idealises him: «If I have before me an Italian model (Matisse here has in mind the «Model» of the Moscow Museum of Modern Western Art)that at the first glance arouses in me a conception of a purely animal being, then I disclose in her essential traits; among the traits of her face those that reflect the character of high importance, that is preserved in every human being» (Notes d'un Peintre) [1].

No less abstract is his treatment of the nude. For Matisse in the 1910's the human figure is merely

_____

[1] At the same time we must note that in the 1900's and 1910's Matisse paints some expressive portraits. When he seriously approaches this problem, he can successfully solve it, as for example in his «Self-Portrait» (1908).

a combination of expressive lines and rhythmic surfaces, points of application of colour energy. In his strongly abstracted, extremely rhythmically moving figures there is a certain resemblance to those in «The Bathers» of Cézanne's last period, which were drawn, as is well known, without the model. Matisse, who makes innumerable studies of the figure, is even less concerned with anatomy than Cézanne. Before everything he seeks expression. He takes exceedingly arbitrary proportions, excessively enlarges his heads, lengthens his necks, shortens or lengthens his limbs and, sometimes generalises his forms, ignoring essential details. For example the left hand figure in «Ball Game» has no chest and no stomach, in place of an instep there is only an amorphous touch of colour. This schematism reaches its completest development in his cubist representations of the naked body in 1917—1918, and also in his murals of 1932—1934. It is true that in the 1920's in Matise, Picasso, Derain and others of the «left», there arises a striving towards greater concreteness, towards a more easily perceived art. This striving, characteristic of the period of capitalist stabilisation, is accompanied by a strengthening of hedonistic elements in their art. Several Matisse portraits of the 1920's speak of a search for character, of an attempt to show real people and not merely decorative, human-like figures. But at this point an obstacle stands in his way, that almost negates his attempts to approach to realistic representation. It is not a question of those inevitable difficulties that the artist meets with when he turns from abstractness to a detailed study of nature. This obstacle is first of all a natural attraction to decorativism still further complicated by a tendency to elegance and eroticism, that is stamped on the latest works of Matisse. In the 1910's he attempted to avoid the usual run of prettiness, even allowing distortions in his pictures, although of course, not to the same extent as Rouault does in his extraordinary female figures. But this tendency is bound up with searches for harmonious beauty. A glance at «Ball Game» and others of his pictures makes one feel that Matisse had memories of Greek reliefs and vase ornaments.

It is characteristic that even in the 1910's Matisse almost never depicts the male nude. His attention is concentrated on the female figure. In his series of «odalisques», Matisse gives a whole gallery of sensitive forms, seated or extended on divans amid gaudy cloths, carpets, flowers and draperies. The erotic element is emphasised in their poses, the elegance of their bodies and finally by the fact that they are half nude and posed in the intimate surroundings of a living room. Matisse catered to the demands of the post-war bourgeoisie, at a time when eroticism became strongly rooted in life, in literature, music, the dance and in prevailing fashions.

Matisse, however, did not succeed in giving a sufficiently concrete image in this not very elevated genre. The Odalisques of Ingres, the harems of Delacroix are deeply felt and convincingly rendered. Matisse odalisques are always just models, one feels only too keenly that they are posed, and at the same time they are not real enough. Strange as it may seem, Matisse, who was always striving for abstraction, could not in this case get away from the model. Sometimes he frankly discloses his method, titling other works of this period (the 1920's) simply «Model», «Nude», «Models at Rest», etc., and in these latter studies of the nude figure, or in his still-lifes, he retains all the expressiveness of his earlier canvases, he is much more convincing. In other «Odalisques» there is a touch of «prettiness» even in their very colouring. This is already not the superficially perceived East that he painted in his Moroccan pictures, but an East artificially concocted in the studio with the help of simple stage props — harem costumes, shawls, jewels, rugs.

But this subordinatian of his art to the requirements of the post war bourgeoisie did not, thanks to his tremendous talent, stop Matisse's growth as a painter. In the 1920's Matisse not only lost nothing of his early daring and freshness but was able to undertake a new approach to the problems of colour and form. He is already not satisfied with his former decorativism and aims at integrated painting. We must add that eclecticism is foreign to his art. Unlike Picasso and Derain he does not take as mentor now one and now another Old Master, but steadfastly travels his own individual path.

Matisse's latest period is characterised by a heightened interest in volume and space. In the 1910's, dreaming of big mural paintings, he strove to integrate his objects with the flat surface of the canvas and reduced them to two-dimensional forms (as in «Dinner Table», «The Dance», and others). But his interest in mass was preserved even in these years, as he once said: «The means in painting do not play the great role that they are usually supposed to. I am not

62

bound to what I do. Without the slightest hesitation I would discontinue painting if I could express myself more completely in any other medium. And so in order to express form, I sometimes take to sculpture, which allows me to get right around the object and study it better, instead of standing before a flat surface» (F. Fels). Thus he often devoted himself to sculpture, and attained in this realm more significant results than most other modern French painters not excepting Derain, Modigliani and Picasso. In his earlier sculptural work, that is angular and geometricised, Matisse strongly emphasises mass. His figures are not monolithic, but made up of sharply accented, conflicting elements of mass. Matisse loves to picture his statuettes in his still-lifes and interiors. In the 1920's he carefully models his pencil and dry-brush drawings, and in his paintings he also models his objects by means of local colour.

Matisse's approach to the solution of the spatial problems in the 1910's appears to be somewhat contradictory. On the one hand his guiding principle in decorating the canvas surface would seem to exclude the representation of three-dimensional space. The more finished canvases, both of this and the next period, are built up of big decorative bands, rhythmically dividing the canvas surface either horizontally or vertically. It would be incorrect to identify these colour surfaces with spatial planes, since this would mean confusing the building up of space, with the organisation of the colour surface, i. e., with the accenting of different elements of a decorative whole. Matisse's «background» and «foreground» colours only serve this latter end — and this is the method of differentiating colour met with in any rug. It would be a complete confusion of meanings to consider the background of a rug or a Matisse's still-life as an element of depth or space, or the ornamental spots of colour as «objects» in the true meaning of the word.

In other landscapes of the Fauve period, when Matisse utilises a conception of three-dimensional space, he gives the effect of distance but only up to a certain point, for simultaneously he almost negates the significance of these depths by his interplay of colour surfaces as for example in «Tangiers». In his excellent «Zorah on the Terrace» he consciously omits the line of the floor and the corners of the wall; the female figure seems to hang in the air. Following the example of the Persians in other canvases («The Music Lesson» for instance) he treats the first and second planes of the picture alike, employs inverse perspective, makes the figures of the foreground smaller than those of the background, that is, weakens the effect of depth as much as possible. But together with these flattened surfaces in the 1910's we also meet with works in which spacial depth is strongly emphasised. Flat representations of the artist's studio are interspersed with studies of the same studio with well-expressed perspective effects, or still-lifes in which objects are shown foreshortened; but these latter are exceptions. In the 1920's Matisse on the contrary gives depth in his canvases, gives the illusion of three-dimensional form; this even becomes his favourite form of expression. Thus, for example, the «Road to Villacouble» depicts an avenue sharply shortened in perspective and shows

64

View from a Window (Tangiers), 1912.

an automobile receding into the distance. The interiors painted in Nice from 1923—1928 are constructed on the principle of a panorama; in order to accentuate his perspective, Matisse employs a typically baroque method; in the foreground he gives a close-up of some object (an armchair, a violin-case, etc.) and on the second plane a small female figure. But even here Matisse does not forego his former predilection for decorative lines and the ornamental construction of his canvas surface. He fills his pictures with all sorts of stripped or patterned objects. Here we see the open struggle of two opposed principles, and in the 1920's the spatial principle gains the ascendancy. Thanks to his fine artistic sensibility, however, the artist by no means weakens the decorative effect of his pictures. Then again in 1931—1935, Matisse returns to extreme flatness in his murals and easel painting.

The strengthening of the elements of volume and space in his art, in no way, lessened the richness of his colour. This remained as intense as ever, became even more varied. But even these later canvases with their soft and more supple colouring, which is sometimes reminiscent of Renoir, are still built up on sharp contrasts: Take for example his «Woman in an Armchair»[1].

The idea of the picture cannot rouse our interest, it again shows his usual, characterless model, but it is nevertheless interesting as an outstanding example of Matisse's mastery of the art of painting. The body, with its warm lilac shadows, is painted in hot golden

---

[1] Reproduced in Fels' monograph

tones. The background is a magnificent harmony of cold red and delicate rose with warm greens merging into olive. An extremely keen effect is produced by the contrast of the pure cobalt blue of the sky with the brown-black shutters. The whole picture shines, the woman's body is enlivened by a carefully placed spot of sunlight. Here Matisse strives to give not merely the «equivalent of sunlight», but sunlight itself. During the last few years he has painted several pictures with light effects — sunrays, penetrating a half darkened room through the openings of the shutters, or a dark figure on the background of an open window. Finally he approaches the task of depicting atmospheric effects. He sometimes makes use of diffuse form, paints in soft mother-of-pearl tones — sky blue, pale rose, pearl grey, introduces floods of light that dissolve contours and creates delicate gradations of light and shade, and in some pictures he approaches the effects of impressionism.

In this period Matisse endeavours to concentrate in his hands all those powerful artistic means that, in the search for new paths, he discarded twenty five years previously. He strives to overcome pure decorativism and in some of his pictures approaches the problems of integral easel painting — a combination of mass, space and colour problems. With a rich experience of painting he returns to his initial starting point of the 1890's.

Matisse's painting in these latter years is not realistic, it is still full of improvisations and phantasies on the theme of reality. Fundamentally he remains an artist who deforms reality and distorts natural proportions for the sake of colour rhythm. His paintings always lack finish. In one and the same picture one will find a combination of his earlier flat methods of painting with his new methods of treating volume and space, which results sometimes in a lack of balance. While feeling the necessity of representing those elements of reality that he formerly ignored, Matisse nevertheless stops half way. His latest period is filled with contradictions; progress in the sphere of colour is not always accompanied by equivalent attainments in the sphere of form and composition. It is in this latter sphere that Matisse, as a general rule, refrains from too daring experiments. It is here that he holds most closely to Western or Oriental tradition. The objects and colour surfaces of his finished compositions are usually arranged in a wave-like horizontal line traversing the whole width of the picture with rhythmic pauses, in the form of «empty spaces», that is, they essentially follow out the classic tradition. He often develops this tradition in original and unexpected ways. Thus for example his mural «Music» in the Moscow Museum of Modern Western Art is built up on the traditional triangle of the classic masters, but in this case the triangle is placed horizontally with ts apex to the right and with three figures placed opposite the verticals of the figure standing at the left. In his later works Matisse employs the compositional methods of the Persian miniatures and Japanese prints. In the large murals painted for the Barnes Foundation, Matisse presents a very complete composition; despite the sharply accentuated movements, he attains complete balance. All the figures of the murals are united by a great flowing arabesque that serves as their common foundation. These murals are executed on the same theme as «The Dance» in the Moscow Museum of Modern Western Art, but the composition is more complex than that of the spherically constructed «Dance». In the Barnes murals Matisse arrives at schematic stylisation in his drawing in place of the sharp and expressive lines of «The Dance».

In these murals Matisse gets away from reality to a degree that can only be compared with his repudiation of nature and three-dimensional painting in 1906—1908. Now, as then, this is the result of his natural trend to decorativism and abstraction from reality, which is expressed in this case by absolute flatness in his forms, by strongly contrasted colour, a simplification of his palette (the bodies are painted pearl grey, with background in black, rose and blue) and in even more extreme deformation — which leaves arms without hand, and excessively lengthens or narrows different parts of the body.

On the one hand Matisse wished to distinguish his murals as much as possible from the pictures hanging in the same hall, and on the other hand he sought a style that corresponds to the architecture of the gallery. In filling the arches of the vaults with forms, that in part repeat the architectural motive and in part contrast with it, Matisse motivates his distortions as a solution of the specific demands of monumental painting.

«In architectural painting, to which category my mural belongs, the human element must be reduced, if not entirely excluded. I set myself the aim of interlacing painting with architecture, of giving the equi-

68

valent of cement and stone in the mural... My colours, lines and movement give the impression of flight, they force one to forget the proportions of the arches that are slung too low»[1].

Considered in relation to the development of an art style of the modern bourgeoise, the sum of Matisse's many years of work is not very great when compared to the great role played by Cubism. For however we may evaluate Cubism, one thing is certain,— it is a particular historic style that harmonises with contemporary capitalist reality, it is a style as dynamic, unbalanced and disharmonious as decaying capitalism itself. It is a style that despite the disintegration of cubist painting itself, affected architecture, sculpture, the applied arts, poster and book design and became deeply rooted in the life of the modern West. If the logic and simplicity of cubist form reflect the capitalist tendency to rationalisation and economy, then its disjointed, distorted and asymmetrical composition reflects the dominant tendency to self-destruction, contradiction and the fatal antagonisms, lying at the base of this economic system. Thus cubism reflects the complex reality of the imperialist stage of capitalism. Matisse's harmonious decorativeness does not express these strong tendencies. Picasso sees into the depths of phenomena, identifies himself with the tempestuous rhythms and dissonances of the epoch, with its cacaphony and ugliness; Matisse glides over the surface. Enjoying immense popularity, he does not

[1] «Two letters from Henri Matisse»· «Iskusstvo» Moscow. 1934, 4.

create a unified school—he is one of the individualist Fauves-people of a past epoch for whom the highest good is an abstract freedom, understood as an extreme assertion of the ego.

We cannot accept the hedonistic outlook of Matisse, his repudiation of ideas, his unwillingness to strive for deep pictorial realisation and give an adequate reflection of reality. But the positive elements of his painting—powerful, intensive colour, his daring and dynamic treatment of form, mastery of the laws of decorative rhythm—can and must find a corresponding expression in Soviet art which stands before the problems of monumental painting and therefore cannot ignore the heritage of Matisse.

BIBLIOGRAPHY

Henri Mercereau. Henri Matisse and Modern Painting («Zolotoe Runo» 1909, № 6. 17 reproductions).

J. Tugendhold. «The French Collection of S. I. Schukin» («Apollon» 1914, № 1—2, pages 22—28).

P. Pertsov. The Schukin Collection of French Painting. Moscow 1922, pages 86—92.

J. Tugendhold. The First Museum of Modern Western Painting. Moscow 1923, pages 65—76.

A. G. Romm. Henri Matisse. «Iskusstvo» 1934 № 3. A. G. Romm. Henri Matisse. Moscow 1935.

B. Ternovets. Henri Matisse in: Masters of Art on Art. Volume III. Moscow 1934, pp. 369—402.

Henri Matisse. Notes d'un Peintre, Grande Revue, 25/XII 1908.

Marcel Sembat. Henri Matisse. Paris 1920. 16 p. 24 reproductions.

Roland Schacht. Henri Matisse, Dresden 1922. 55 p. 33 reproductions.

E. Faure, J. Romains, Ch. Vidrac. Henri Matisse, Paris 1923. 52 p. 29 reproductions.

Adolph Basler. Henri Matisse, Leipzig 1924, 40 p. 32 reproductions.

Valdemar Georges. Dessins de Henri Matisse. Paris 1925. 20 p. 70 reproductions.

Florent Fels. Henri Matisse, Paris 1929. 49 p. 86 reproductions.

Henri Matisse. 220 reproductions en simili gravure, Editions Cahiers d'Art 1931.

Roger Fry. Henri Matisse, London 1930.

Anthony Bertram. Henri Matisse, London 1931.

Albert C. Barnes and Violette de Mazia. The Art of Henri Matisse, New York. 1933. 464 p., 151 reproductions.

Roger Fry. Henri Matisse. Chroniques du Jour, Paris 1935.

See also: the special number of Cahiers d'Art (1931. № 6) devoted to Matisse. G. Duthuit, «Le Fauvisme», Cahiers d'Art 1929, № 3, 6, 9.

LIST OF ILLUSTRATIONS

ILLUSTRATIONS

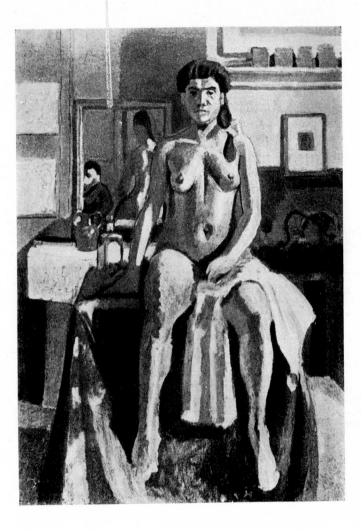

Carmelina, 1901.

Back of a Nude, 1903.

Self. Portrait, 1907.

Spanish Girl with a Tambourine, 1909.

The Joy of Life, 1907.

The Dance, 1909.

The Music, 1910.

Portrait of the Artist's Wife, 1911.

Head of Woman, 1916.

Music Lesson, 1916.

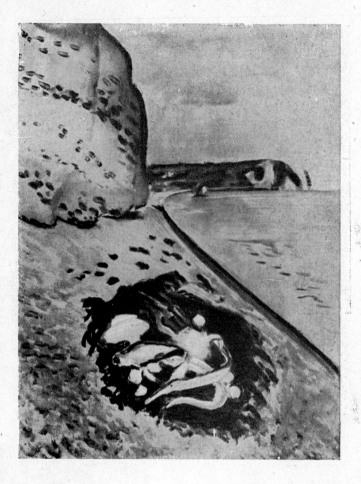

Etretat, the Skate, 1920.

Shrimps, 1921.

Roses, 1925.

Moorish Woman, 1922.

Interior, 1923.

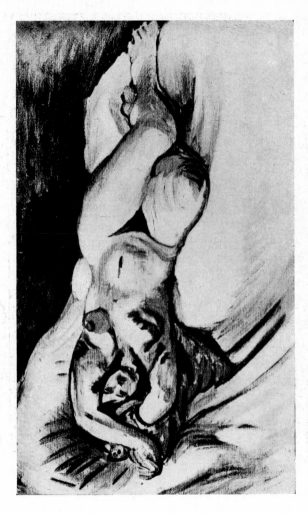

Reclining Nude, 1920.

Woman with an Aquarium, 1924.

Spanish Girl, 1924.

Odalisque in a White Turban, 1926.

Studio at Nice, 1924.

Girl in Yellow, 1929—1931.

Girl with Draped Headdress. Pencil, 1929.

Reclining Woman. Bronze, 1928—1931.

Souvenir de Tahiti (Sketch for a Beauvais tapestry), 1934.

Seated Nude. Pencil, 1933.

The Dance. Murals in the Barnes Foundation, 1931—1933. Fir

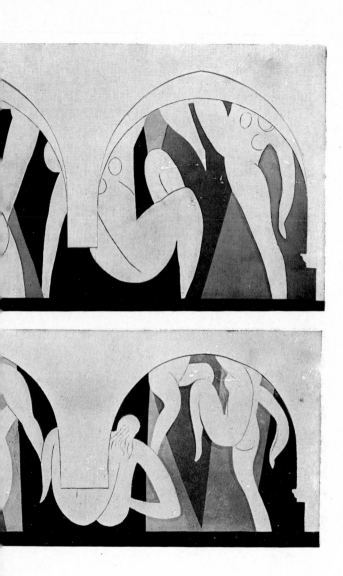

riants.

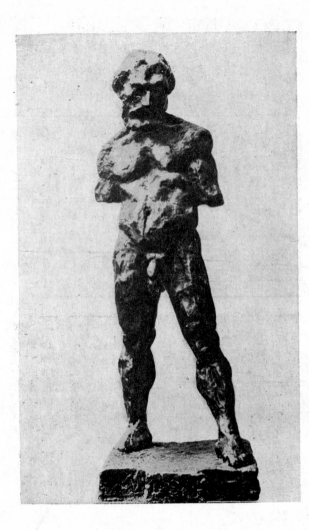

Slave. Bronze, 1900's.

Portrait, 1936.

Printed in Soviet Union